WITH THIS RING

Published by WaterBrook Press

5446 North Academy Boulevard, Suite 200

Colorado Springs, Colorado 80918

A division of Random House, Inc.

ISBN 1-57856-188-4

Printed in the United States of America

1999—First Edition

10 9 8 7 6 5 4 3 2 1

Presented to

_____

ON THIS DAY_____

FROM_____

Where were you, since the beginning of the world?
But now you are here, about me in every space, room,
sunlight, with your heart and arms and the light of your soul.

JOHN JAY CHAPMAN TO WIFE, MINNA,
SEPTEMBER 21, 1891

Heart, *Love*

ARE YOU GREAT ENOUGH FOR A THAT NEVER TIRES?

ALFRED, LORD TENNYSON

Dearly Beloved, WE ARE GATHERED TOGETHER HERE IN THE SIGHT OF GOD, AND IN THE FACE OF THIS COMPANY, TO JOIN TOGETHER THIS MAN AND THIS WOMAN IN HOLY MATRIMONY; WHICH IS... COMMENDED OF SAINT PAUL TO BE HONORABLE AMONG ALL MEN: AND THEREFORE IS NOT BY ANY TO BE ENTERED INTO UNADVISEDLY OR LIGHTLY; BUT REVERENTLY, DISCREETLY, ADVISEDLY, SOBERLY, AND IN THE FEAR OF GOD. INTO THIS HOLY ESTATE THESE TWO PERSONS PRESENT COME NOW TO BE JOINED. IF ANY MAN CAN SHOW JUST CAUSE WHY THEY MAY NOT LAWFULLY BE JOINED TOGETHER, LET HIM NOW SPEAK, OR ELSE HEREAFTER FOREVER HOLD HIS PEACE. THE BOOK OF COMMON PRAYER

𝓘 DO LOVE
YOU SO

IT'S LIKE A WELL,
SO DEEP
THAT IF YOU WENT
TO THE VERY BOTTOM,
YOU WOULD SEE STARS.

VICTORIA SACKVILLE-WEST

Simple Words. *"I do"* spoken twice. A lifetime of promise within two tiny words. And with these words we write the opening sentence of our marriage. Side by side, hand in hand, we declare in bold strokes our single-hearted allegiance: "This is my love—there will be no other."

Over the centuries, millions of couples have committed themselves to each other using the traditional wedding ceremony found in the *Book of Common Prayer*. Whether spoken in a chapel or whispered on a hillside, these vows are sacred words. Powerful promises. They are not to be spoken lightly nor abandoned when the going gets tough. So help us God.

Phrase by phrase, promise upon promise, we write a covenant linking our life with another.

Will you? Can you? Do you? The answer comes as sure as the sunrise, bursting through our hearts and dancing out into the sacred space where we stand—Yes, I will. I can. And I do!

With This Ring: Promises to Keep is dedicated to all who dare write a forever-love story in a world filled with dime-a-dozen romances. "Heart, are you great enough for a love that never tires?" Lord Tennyson asks. The veil, the tuxedo, the flowers—they make up the wedding. Patience, kindness, gentleness—they make up the marriage.

"I pronounce you husband and wife. You may kiss your bride."

These are the final words of the ceremony and the first words of our life together.

The next page lies bare. And in our hands, we hold the pen.

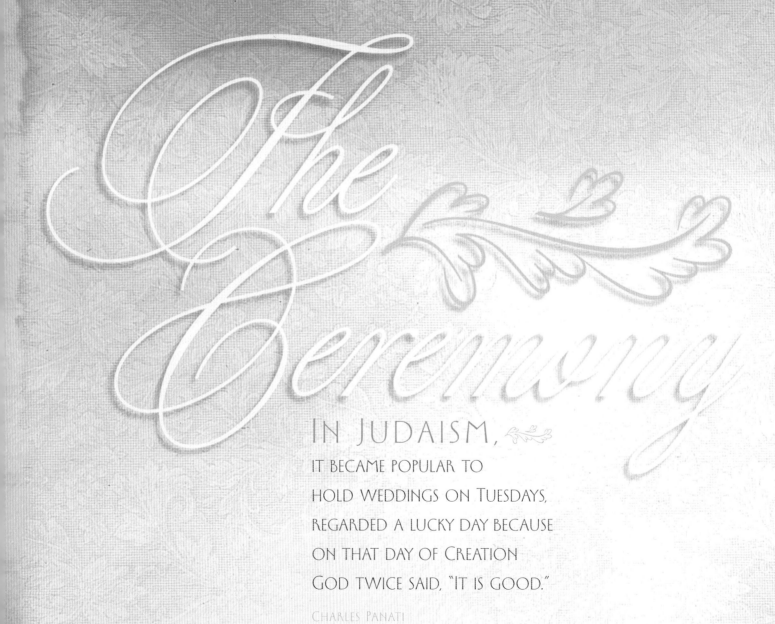

"SO THEY ARE NO LONGER TWO, BUT ONE. THEREFORE WHAT GOD HAS JOINED TOGETHER, LET MAN NOT SEPARATE."
MATTHEW 19:6

The Ceremony

IN JUDAISM,

IT BECAME POPULAR TO

HOLD WEDDINGS ON TUESDAYS,

REGARDED A LUCKY DAY BECAUSE

ON THAT DAY OF CREATION

GOD TWICE SAID, "IT IS GOOD."

CHARLES PANATI
SACRED ORIGINS OF THE PROFOUND

She walks toward him in quiet beauty. His destiny, his life, all wrapped up in this woman soon to be his wife. The music softens and his anxiety fades as he looks into her face, full of serenity. And in that single moment he knows—this is right. Like a wandering stream finally reaching the sea, his heart has finally found a resting place.

It isn't enough for a couple to say, "I love you." It isn't enough simply to live together. A love like this cannot be contained in a cardboard box, which disintegrates with time and disinterest. This love is too precious. This love requires the golden chalice of commitment. This love requires a ceremony—a sacred assembly of all those we know, called to witness and hold us accountable to all we say. Before God and humankind, we speak holy vows—pounding earthly stakes to form new boundaries and open new territory. From this day forward, we are one till death do us part.

Historically, marriage vows were irrevocable. Once spoken, they were never to be broken. Those who dared go back on their word paid dearly, even to death. While vows may have lost their potency in today's fickle society, they still echo in the heavenlies. As God is our witness, we will be called to give account for every word we've spoken.

> RITUALS ARE
> IMPORTANT.
> NOWADAYS IT'S
> NOT HIP TO BE
> MARRIED. I'M
> NOT INTERESTED
> IN BEING HIP.
> JOHN LENNON

We are gathered here

A HAPPY
MARRIAGE IS
A LONG
CONVERSATION
THAT ALWAYS
SEEMS TOO
SHORT.
ANDRÉ MAUROIS

A DREAM COME *True.* It had never seemed right to Jim Porter. A woman like Patty deserved all the frills and lace little girls dream of in a wedding. Instead, they had been married in a simple ceremony with four friends looking on. Patty had worn a borrowed wedding gown. There was no fancy reception. For years Jim had dreamed of making their twenty-fifth anniversary the wedding they never had. But Lou Gehrig's disease changed all that.

In February 1995, the doctors told Jim he had six to twelve months to live. Lou Gehrig's is a degenerative nervous system disorder without any cure, a mixture of pain and paralysis that in 80 percent of cases leads to death within two years.

But Jim Porter beat the odds. Two years later he was still alive. And so was his dream.

Without Patty knowing, Jim began piecing together a tribute to the woman he loved. For someone in perfect health, a wedding is a giant undertaking. But Jim refused to let his trembling hands and increasing paralysis stop him.

When he and his teenage daughters couldn't find bridesmaids' dresses they liked, Jim traded a copier for his sister's sewing machine and sewed the off-the-shoulder burgundy satin dresses himself. To his sister's amazement, his seams were nearly perfect.

Never mind the fact Jim Porter had never sewed in his life. "I knew there was a talent," he jokes.

Flowers. Music. A cake. A photographer. Jim had thought of everything. Even Patty's dress. He and the girls shopped for months looking for the perfect gown. Jim unveiled all his plans the night before their twenty-fourth anniversary.

"I have no guarantee I will be around next year," Jim explained to Patty, who was overwhelmed by the extent of his love and the detail of his planning. "My only disappointment is that I didn't get to make your wedding gown."

The following evening Jim and Patty Porter stood together in the gentle candlelight of the Precious Moments Chapel in Carthage, Missouri. Friends and family watched through tears as Jim and Patty again exchanged the vows they'd first spoken so many years before. The ceremony was hushed and holy, yet filled with joy.

"The whole thing was such a picture of Jim's love for me," Patty says. "And yet it wasn't a surprise. He's been loving me like this for twenty-four years." Jim Porter had created the crowning moment of years of cherishing the woman God had given him.

Here he is…, Patty thought as she gazed at Jim through a mist of veil and tears, *loving me again!*

matrimony....

AN IDEAL
WIFE IS ANY
WOMAN
WHO HAS
AN IDEAL
HUSBAND.

BOOTH TARKINGTON

WHO GIVETH THIS WOMAN

There are only two lasting bequests we can hope to give our children.
One of these is roots, the other wings.

HODDING CARTER

GIVING THE *Bride* AWAY. Courted by two suitors, Helene, the beautiful daughter of Maximilian II, king of Germany in the sixteenth century, was unable to choose between the handsome German baron and the dashing Spaniard. When the two proposed a duel for her hand, the prospective father-in-law suggested a less deadly contest. Handing each man a gunnysack, the king promised to give his daughter in marriage to the first man who could bag the other.

After wrestling nearly an hour, Baron Von Talbert finally succeeded in stuffing his opponent into the bag. He lifted the bulging sack and carried it across the room. Dropping it at Helene's feet, the baron made his proposal, which was immediately accepted by the fair maiden.

Helene was one of the lucky ones—she had a say in the man she married. In primitive times, a man didn't bother asking for a pretty girl's hand in marriage. He just took it. The honeymoon is said to have evolved from the need to hide from the angry fathers and brawny brothers of kidnapped brides. After a month or so, the newlywed couple came out of hiding. The groom made a payment suitable for the loss of a daughter, thus appeasing his offended in-laws and allowing him and his blushing bride to get on with happily ever after.

The marriage-by-capture approach faded as civilization grew and "Me, Tarzan—you, Jane" gave way to "Father knows best." Arranged marriages took center stage with many anxious parents betrothing their children while still in the cradle. It wasn't until the tenth century that women gained the right to choose their husbands according to their own judgment. Yet the approval of parents was important, just as it is today.

When my husband-to-be approached my father for permission to marry me, there were no other suitors begging for my hand and so, sadly, no need for a wrestling match. I've been told the conversation went something like this: "Cliff, I'd like to ask for your daughter's hand in marriage," John said. "But if you don't mind, I'd like the rest of her as well!"

Legally, John didn't need my parents' permission to marry me. But in honoring my father, he honored me, opening a door of loving communication and support that remains today. We received their blessing, a gift which was and is priceless to me. In their approval, I found God's confirmation and the assurance that this was no guessing game. I'd truly captured the right man for me.

And I didn't even need a gunnysack.

LABAN AND BETHUEL ANSWERED, "THIS IS FROM THE LORD....HERE IS REBEKAH. TAKE HER AND GO. AND LET HER BECOME THE WIFE OF YOUR MASTER'S SON, AS THE LORD HAS DIRECTED."...SO THEY CALLED REBEKAH AND ASKED HER. "WILL YOU GO WITH THIS MAN?" "I WILL GO." SHE SAID. Genesis 24:50-51,58

O BE MARRIED TO THIS MAN?

The Bride . . .
Floating all white
beside her
father in the morning
shadow of trees,
her veil flowing with
laughter.

D. H. LAWRENCE

AFFIRMATION OF THE

Betrothal Pledge

May heaven grant you in all things your heart's desire—husband, house, and a happy, peaceful home. For there is nothing better in this world than that a man and woman, sharing the same ideas, keep house together. It discomforts their enemies and makes the hearts of their friends glad—but they themselves know more about it than anyone.

HOMER

ODYSSEY

IT ALL *begins* WITH A QUESTION: Will you marry me? One woman whispers, "Yes," while another declares, "You bet!" I know of one excited but jittery woman who hauled off and punched her beau when he popped the question. When he finally came to, she was bending over him, repeating, "Yes, yes, yes, I'll marry you!"

In biblical times, the engagement was as solemn and important as the wedding ceremony is today. Rather than asking the girl himself (possibly fearing a left hook), a man or his representative approached the father of the woman he wanted to marry. If the father agreed, the two haggled the bride price and other particulars. Once they came to an agreement, a date for the betrothal ceremony was set.

In a service separate from the actual wedding, the couple came, often meeting for the first time, to speak the binding words of the betrothal pledge. Rings were exchanged in the presence of witnesses and the promise sealed by a kiss.

From that moment the bride and groom were betrothed, an Old English word that means "for truth." They were bound to one another in an irreversible contract, although the marriage itself might not take place for several years. Each one signed the *ketubah*, an ornate legal document still used today in Jewish ceremonies. Only death or divorce could nullify the agreement.

Eventually the betrothal ceremony combined with the wedding, forming the marriage service we celebrate today. Marrying for love instead of money eliminated the need for matchmakers, middlemen, and elaborate legal documents. Though a ring is still given upon engagement, the ancient vows proclaiming the couple's free choice to marry aren't spoken till the day they wed.

I THINK A MAN AND A WOMAN SHOULD CHOOSE EACH OTHER FOR LIFE, FOR THE SIMPLE REASON THAT A LONG LIFE IS BARELY ENOUGH FOR A MAN AND WOMAN TO UNDERSTAND EACH OTHER, AND TO UNDERSTAND IS TO LOVE. J.B. Yeats

Wilt thou have this woman to be thy wedded wife . . .

THE *Wonder* OF IT ALL. It was a match made in heaven. It had to be. For a man like John to choose to spend his life with a woman like me, well, it seemed miraculous to me.

For a split moment, I wondered if it was all some marvelous mirage. There I stood, in my childhood church, marrying my childhood dream. I'd met John when I was thirteen. So tall and handsome, he was everything I'd ever hoped for. But alas, he was nearly four years older, and as everyone knows, sixteen-year-olds-going-on-seventeen-year-olds never look at thirteen-year-olds. So I worshiped from afar. He was the sun, the moon, the stars; and I, the earthbound mole.

Then one day, when I was sixteen-going-on-seventeen, some kind of holy chemistry erupted between us, and I knew he was the one. He agreed. Three years later, we stood at the altar.

MY LIFE
HAS BEEN THE
AWAITING YOU,
YOUR FOOTFALL
WAS MY OWN
HEART'S BEAT.
PAUL VALÉRY

"Will you take this woman to be your wedded wife?" The question hung in the air like gossamer stretched thin between us. A sudden terror rose in my throat. What if he said no? What if this was some cruel dream and I suddenly awoke to darkness?

But then, like a soft, silken ribbon, his gaze caught mine and pulled me in. There was no fear in his eyes, no doubt, no double-mindedness. Only a tender determination. And tears. In the sparkling blue depths of his eyes, I caught a glimpse of all that I could be—a reflection of what he saw when he looked at me. His choice was no cosmic fluke. This man loved me. Me.

Wedded wife. The word *wed* comes from the same root word as *wage*. It goes back to the tradition of the "bride price." When a man wanted to marry a woman, he was required to pay a certain amount of money or goods prescribed by her father. The more desirable the woman, the higher the price.

I HAVE NOTHING TO *Share* WITH YOU BUT MY LIFE.
PETER MCWILLIAMS

There's always a price to pay when you love. And I'm afraid there have been times in our seventeen years of marriage when John has paid dearly. Times when what I could be contrasts painfully with what I am. And yet, he continues to love me. Me.

The tender strands of his love embrace me. They constrain me, refusing to let me go. They uphold me when I'm weary of trying to stand. "She belongs to me," they say.

"She is my wedded wife."

WILL YOU BE MARRIED?

I feel sad when I don't see you. Be married, why won't you? And come to live with me. I will make you as happy as I can. You shall not be obliged to work hard; and when you are tired, you may lie in my lap and I will sing you to rest. I will play you a tune upon the violin as often as you ask and as well as I can; and leave off smoking, if you say so.... I would always be very kind to you, I think, because I love you so well. I will not make you bring in wood and water, or feed the pig, or milk the cow, or go to the neighbours to borrow milk. Will you be married?

LETTER FROM A SUITOR
IN NINETEENTH-CENTURY AMERICA

My wife would have blond hair and green eyes. She'd be funny but serious sometimes. She'd be smart, pretty, and nice. We would go to parties once a month and go to baseball games. We would especially have fun. She'd give me a kiss every day and love me. She'd listen when I talk. She would brag about me a little. We would spend ten minutes talking to each other each day. We would have three children, Bobby, Amy, and Rick. She would be my best friend.

BOY, AGE ELEVEN
TAKE TIME TO PLAY CHECKERS

to live together after God's ordinance

THERE IS NO
SURPRISE MORE
MAGICAL
THAN THE
SURPRISE OF
BEING LOVED:
IT IS GOD'S
FINGER ON
MAN'S
SHOULDER.

CHARLES MORGAN

in the holy estate of matrimony?

That I may come near to her, draw me nearer to *Thee* than to her;

That I may know her, make me to know Thee more than her;

That I may love her with the perfect love of a perfectly whole heart,

Cause me to love Thee more than her and most of all. Amen. Amen.

That nothing may be between me and her, be Thou between us, every moment.

That we may be constantly together, draw us into separate loneliness with Thyself.

And when we meet breast to breast, my God, let it be on Thy own. Amen. Amen.

TEMPLE GAIRDNER

A Marriage

You are holding up a ceiling
with both arms. It is very heavy,
but you must hold it up, or else
it will fall down on you. Your arms
are tired, terribly tired,
and, as the day goes on, it feels
as if either your arms or the ceiling
will soon collapse.

But then,
unexpectedly,
something wonderful happens:
someone,
a man or a woman,
walks into the room
and holds their arms up
to the ceiling beside you.

So you finally get
to take down your arms.
You feel the relief of respite,
the blood flowing back
to your fingers and arms.
And when your partner's arms tire,
you hold up your own
to relieve him again.

And it can go on like this
for many years
without the house falling.

Michael C. Blumenthal

Come what may. . .

Kim Carpenter had never seen anything more beautiful in his life. The day he had waited for was finally here. Teal ribbon and pink roses lined the candlelit chapel where he and 250 guests stood. But Kim saw only his bride. A stab of pure joy pierced his heart as Krickitt met him at the altar, her incredible blue eyes mirroring the excitement and love in his own eyes.

Every detail of the ceremony is seared into Kim's memory. The words he spoke to Krickitt were broken by emotion and filled with love. "I will love, comfort, and cherish you.... "

Of that day several years ago Krickitt remembers nothing. It isn't a case of bridal jitters or excitement overload. The wedding is gone—wiped from the keepsake book of Krickitt's memory by the nearly fatal car crash she and Kim were in just ten weeks after their wedding. Eighteen months of Krickitt's life before the wedding and four months after have disappeared into the mist of a coma and brain injury. Gone as well are the memories of her and Kim's courtship, love, and marriage.

Kim hardly recognized his wife "she was so messed up." Though he had several injuries of his own, he drove through the night to the hospital to which his wife had been airlifted. As he held her pale, limp hand, he whispered, "Hang in there, babe. We're going to get through this."

The doctors put Krickitt's chance of survival at less than 1 percent, but people began to pray. Ten days after the accident, Krickitt started to regain consciousness. Kim watched anxiously as his wife emerged from the foggy coma.

"What year is it?" the nurse asked three weeks after the accident.

"Nineteen sixty-five." It was 1993.

Other questions followed. Some Krickitt answered right, others wrong. But there was one question Kim wasn't sure he wanted answered.

"Who's your husband?"

Krickitt paused a moment, then said, "I'm not married."

It was a blow Kim will never forget.

After many months, Krickitt finally moved home, and she and Kim began the process of reassembling their lives. But nothing was the same. "So, how did I do this 'wife thing'?" Krickitt asked. "Did I cook dinner? Did I make you a lunch?"

"I felt more like Krickitt's father than her husband," Kim says. "We had to start over." And start over they did. They began dating again. He had wooed her once, and Kim was determined to win her again. "I had said my vows before God—'in sickness and in health'— and I meant them."

As for Krickitt, Kim was just a man who stood beside a woman in a wedding photograph who looked like her. "But I knew that if I loved him before, God could help me love him again."

"Two and a half years ago, I made a vow before God, and as I stated then, I state now with greater love and desire. I promise to defend our love and hold it in highest regard. I promise to be forgiving, understanding, and patient. I promise to tend to your every need. I promise to respect and honor you fully."

KIM CARPENTER AT SECOND CEREMONY

Kim's plan began to work. They spent Saturday afternoons at the lake together, cutting across whitecaps on Wave Runners, then whiled away the evenings laughing and talking about the day over pizza—Canadian bacon. Romantic dinners and strolling through Wal-Mart hand in hand initiated a new legacy of love. Krickitt found herself thinking how she'd miss him if he were gone. As for Kim—well, he certainly wasn't feeling like her father anymore.

On Valentine's Day, 1996, three years after the accident, Kim proposed once again. Krickitt accepted.

The ceremony was simple yet sacred. The tiny log chapel in the Sangre de Cristo mountains near their New Mexico home was filled with close friends and relatives. Their faces lit only by lanterns, Kim looked into the beautiful blue eyes of the woman he loved. Then, each after the other, they repeated the vows that had held them together. Vows that had been tested by fire and found true.

To new couples and to those about to be married, Kim and Krickitt Carpenter offer this advice: "Read your vows carefully. Repeat them twenty times. Look between the lines, understand the promises you make. Fill in the spaces with every possibility, and then, if you're ready, say them. But know this: You may be called to live them out in ways you never imagined."

LOVE IS NOT A
POSSESSION BUT A
GROWTH. THE HEART
IS A LAMP WITH JUST
OIL ENOUGH TO BURN
FOR AN HOUR, AND
IF THERE BE NO OIL TO
PUT IN AGAIN, ITS LIGHT
WILL GO OUT. GOD'S
GRACE IS THE OIL THAT
FILLS THE LAMP OF LOVE.

HENRY WARD BEECHER

and, forsaking all others,

YOU HAVE BEEN
SUCH LIGHT TO
ME THAT OTHER
WOMEN HAVE
BEEN YOUR
SHADOWS.

WENDELL BERRY

Diamonds IN YOUR BACKYARD. A legend says that long ago in ancient Persia there lived a man named Ali Hafed. He owned a large farm filled with lush orchards, acres of grainfields, and beautiful gardens. His wife was lovely, and his children brought him great pleasure. Ali Hafed was quite content.

One day a priest came to visit. "Diamonds are to be desired above all else," the wizened old man told Ali, his eyes vibrant, his hands expressive. "If you have diamonds, you'll never want for anything."

The priest's words took root, and Ali became consumed with the translucent jewels—their fire, their depth, their worth. Soon Ali Hafed sold his farm and left his family to search the world for the finest diamonds. He would have them, no matter the cost.

Ali's quest took him all through Europe and down into Africa, but he found nothing that satisfied him. Before long, his money was gone, and his dreams of diamonds lay as shredded as the rags that clothed his body.

Hopeless and discouraged, Ali Hafed stood at the edge of a stormy Barbary Coast bay. Whipped by wind and rain, he stared at a giant tidal wave approaching the shore. But instead of running for safety, Ali calmly walked into the rolling surf and embraced the wave, ending his life.

The man who had purchased Ali Hafed's farm was watering his camel at the garden brook one day. The sun hung brilliant in the cloudless sky as the camel thrust his snout deep into the shallow water. Suddenly a bright glint in the white sand caught the farmer's eye. He bent down and gently brushed the sand away, revealing glistening stones. Diamonds. Scores and scores of diamonds.

There in the brook lay the beginnings of the most magnificent diamond mine in the history of humankind: the Golconda. From its depths would come the largest crown jewels in the world.

Ali Hafed had gone searching the world for diamonds, while all along, the largest and the very best lay under his feet.

The rarest, most beautiful diamonds are found in our own backyards. Don't run looking elsewhere. Take time to whisk away the sand that obscures your treasure. The sand of time and busyness. The silt of ingratitude. Let the water of forgiveness wash away the irritating granules of habit and personality that tend to rub the wrong way.

You'll discover diamonds. Scores and scores of diamonds. Right in your own backyard.

ABOVE ALL ELSE, GUARD YOUR HEART,

FOR IT IS THE WELLSPRING OF LIFE...

MAKE LEVEL PATHS FOR YOUR FEET

AND TAKE ONLY WAYS THAT ARE FIRM.

DO NOT SWERVE TO THE RIGHT OR THE LEFT;

KEEP YOUR FOOT FROM EVIL.

PROVERBS 4:23,26-27

The Vows

MARRIAGE IS NO JOKE;

IT IS NOT LIKE RICE

WHICH CAN BE

SPAT OUT IF IT IS

TOO HOT.

Philippine Proverb

Building a marriage is like building a house: You must begin with a strong foundation. Before you can hammer and nail or prep and paint, you must pour cement footings. Unseen when the house is finished, these underground footings keep your home secure.

In earthquake-plagued California, the building codes require even more. When one church set out to build a new sanctuary, they discovered they couldn't simply pour a slab of cement. For months they had to drill holes into the earth thirty feet deep, down to bedrock. After placing steel rebars inside, they filled the holes with tons of cement. Finally they were ready to pour the slab that would form the floor of their new building. All that work—all that money!—for something no one could see and no one would notice. Until the next "Big One," that is.

When the earth shakes, it's better to have your footings on solid rock than on shifting sand. Like the children's church song says, we need to be wise. Because you can count on one thing in this life: The rains are going to come. Your earth will eventually tremble, and your house had better stand.

Wedding vows are pilings that reach down to the bedrock of integrity in our lives. Like concrete and rebars, they anchor the visible to the unshakable. They are simple promises, made of rock and mud and fire-driven steel. But when we pour the foundation of our future upon them, our marriage won't shift or falter.

These are not easy promises. It's no mistake that *maturity* and *matrimony* come from the same Latin word. As Joseph Barth said, "Marriage is our last, best chance to grow up."

These are not ordinary promises. They marry earth and heaven. For when we pledge our fidelity to one another, God stands as witness to our words. And he doesn't take his job lightly.

Knit your hearts with an unslipping knot.
WILLIAM SHAKESPEARE

I take thee to be my

GOD
BROUGHT
YOU TO ME,
SWEET LOVER,
AND I THINK
HE RAISED ME
TO BE OF
USE TO YOU.

CHRISTINE DE PISAN

He's more myself than I am. Whatever our souls are made of, his and mine are the same. . . . If all else perished, and he remained, I should still continue to be; and if all else remained, and he were annihilated, the Universe would turn to a mighty stranger. . . . . He's always, always in my mind: not as a pleasure . . . but as my own being.

EMILY BRONTË
WUTHERING HEIGHTS

wedded husband...

You are my husband.
My feet shall run because of you.
My feet dance because of you.
My heart shall beat because of you.
My eyes see because of you.
My mind thinks because of you.
And I shall love because of you.

ESKIMO LOVE SONG

in sickness and in health...

TRANSFORMING *Love.* Have you ever seen transforming love? I have. I've seen it in my parents' lifelong infatuation with each other, and I saw it again ten years ago in an elderly couple on a warm September evening after church choir practice.

Jean was a gray-haired woman who sang alto. Quiet and unassuming, she tended to blend into the background. She came and went, sang and left. I guess I never truly saw Jean until the day I met her husband, Al, as he picked her up from choir. From that moment, my perception of Jean was forever altered.

"Isn't she something?" Al said, nudging me with an elbow as he smiled and winked at his bride of thirty years. "That woman brings me so much joy."

Pale, quiet Jean did something I would never have expected. She blushed. Al went on applauding her attributes, building her up with his words. And she began to blossom. Right there before my eyes.

A prolific poet, Al asked if he could quote me a poem about his wife, and I said, "Of course! You must!"

"Oh, Al...," she muttered, embarrassed yet pleased.

I don't remember the words of his poem, but the beauty I saw unfold from deep within Jean I shall never forget. It changed the lowly alto into a glowing madonna and one of the most beautiful women I've ever seen.

Transforming love. The kind that lasts despite time and age, sagging lips and flabby hips. The kind that sticks around when we're not as wonderful as we could be or should be.

The kind of love that still softly glows, though her lover and his poems have since been silenced by the ravages of Alzheimer's disease. In the three short years since I'd seen them last, Jean's vibrant husband had disappeared, leaving an empty shell. My eyes filled with tears as I expressed my sympathy and how hard it must be.

"It's not hard to love," Jean told me, bending down to tuck in a lap quilt around the emaciated legs of her beloved Al. She kissed him softly on the cheek. "Not when you've been loved like I've been loved."

We are each of us angels with only one wing.
And we can only fly
embracing each other.
LUCIANO DE CRESCENZO

to have and
to cherish...

LET ME BE *Your Mirror.* On their honeymoon Bill and Pam Farrel were preparing for an evening out. Bill was ready and waiting for Pam. He lay on the hotel bed, content, watching his lovely new wife fuss with her hair and congratulating himself on his good taste in women. When Pam began to criticize her physical attributes, nothing Bill said seemed to comfort her.

"Inside I was becoming frustrated," Bill writes in their book *Love to Love You!* "After all, she was criticizing my wife!

Love IS AN ACT OF ENDLESS FORGIVENESS,
A *tender look* WHICH BECOMES A HABIT.

PETER USTINOV

"I got up and walked toward Pam. I wrapped my arms around her and gave her a reassuring hug. Then I stepped back, took her face tenderly in my hands, and said, 'Pam, let me be your mirror. You are gorgeous! Let me reflect back to you the beautiful woman you are. If we have to throw all the mirrors in our house away, we will. From now on, I will be your mirror!'"

That is the gift we bring to marriage when we bring the very best love—the purest Godlike, love-your-wife-as-Christ-loves-the-church love. It is in the mirror of forever love that we see ourselves and each other most clearly. Both the good and the bad.

We offer unconditional acceptance, resisting the urge to change or manipulate one another. Gently, honestly, we peel away our masks, revealing weaknesses and vulnerabilities. Then with tender hands we reach to cover one another's oh-so-visible imperfections with love.

And we whisper, "Let me be your mirror. Let me reflect back to you the beauty of who you are."

PARENTS

David Littlefield

Sharen Littlefield

David and Judith Koechel

GRANDPARENTS

Henry and Betty Littlefield

Henry and Karen Steele

Wilson and Georgia Brown

CELEBRANT

Stephen Richards

BEST MAN

Stacy Neubauer
FRIEND OF GROOM

MAID OF HONOR

Tyanne Barsness
FRIEND OF BRIDE

BRIDESMAIDS

Jennifer Littlefield
SISTER OF BRIDE

Emily Littlefield
SISTER OF BRIDE

GROOMSMEN

Scott Bertelson
FRIEND OF GROOM

Perry Duff Smith Jr.
BROTHER IN LAW OF GROOM

Mike Caspersen
FRIEND OF GROOM

IT IS A LITTLE
EMBARRASSING
THAT AFTER
FORTY-FIVE YEARS
OF RESEARCH
AND STUDY,
THE BEST ADVICE
I CAN GIVE TO
PEOPLE IS TO BE A
LITTLE KINDER TO
EACH OTHER.
ALDOUS HUXLEY

The Love Chapter

If I had the gift of being able to speak in other languages without learning them

and could speak in every language there is in all of heaven and earth,

but didn't love others, I would only be making noise.

If I had the gift of prophecy and knew all about what is going to happen in the future,

knew everything about *everything*, but didn't love others, what good would it do?

Even if I had the gift of faith so that I could speak to a mountain and make it move,

I would still be worth nothing at all without love.

If I gave everything I have to poor people, and if I were burned

alive for preaching the Gospel but didn't love others,

it would be of no value whatever.

Love is very patient and kind, never jealous or envious,

never boastful or proud, never haughty or selfish or rude.

Love does not demand its own way.

It is not irritable or touchy.

It does not hold grudges and will hardly even notice when others do it wrong.

It is never glad about injustice, but rejoices whenever truth wins out.

If you love someone, you will be loyal to him no matter what the cost.

You will always believe in him, always expect the best of him,

and always stand your ground in defending him.

All the special gifts and powers from God will someday come to an end,

but love goes on forever.

I CORINTHIANS 13:1-8 (TLB)

till death do us part.

FOREVER AND *Always*. Of all the strange places for love to show up. Cupid on his worst day would have had enough sense to point his bow elsewhere.

She was a direct descendent of Jonathan Edwards, the great preacher. He was a rough-and-tumble cowboy who'd left home at twelve years of age to bust broncos. She was quiet. He was loud and boisterous. Definitely opposites. And attract they did.

When Ray Weaver caught a glimpse of Rena Edwards, the local preacher's daughter, he knew he would marry her. It was the start of a love affair that lasted over six decades.

I saw the depth of this unlikely love one April evening over wieners and sauerkraut. Newly engaged to their grandson John, I looked forward to meeting the couple that had so influenced his life.

At ninety years of age, Grandpa had been caring for his paralyzed sweetheart for over two years. A stroke had completely silenced the quiet woman, leaving her paralyzed with only her eyes and one curled fist to communicate.

"She's taken care of me for over sixty years," Grandpa informed the family when they'd initially suggested a nursing home. "God's given me this chance to minister to her, and I ain't gonna miss it."

It hadn't been easy. The hot dogs were cold in the middle and the sauerkraut lukewarm, but we feasted on Grandpa's cuisine and dry humor. Grandma's pale blue eyes sparked as she looked from her lover to her grandson as they bantered back and forth. Now and then Grandpa reached over and put his huge spotted hand over her tiny curled one, patting it gently as he told another whopper.

When Grandma passed away the next year, Grandpa was lost. He didn't want to be a burden to anyone. His two sons took him on a trip back to the old homestead in Nebraska and to Wyoming to see where he broke broncos.

It was there that Grandpa got his lifelong wish. He'd always said if he didn't go in the Rapture, he wanted to die in Wyoming with his boots on. Three weeks after his dear Rena went to be with Jesus, Ray Weaver died just outside of Douglas, Wyoming, with his boots on.

I can just imagine him standing at the pearly gates, holding his beautiful wife with one hand, the dusty old cowboy hat he always wore with the other. And after three years of silence, I wouldn't be surprised if the first words out of his sweetheart's lips were, "Ray, wipe those feet. You're messing up the streets of gold!"

Why? the angels wondered. Never had such an honor been given. And yet somehow they understood. The heart of Creator was so large it ached to love. The adoration of angels and their unrestrained praise filled his ears but failed to touch his heart. He longed for love. Not worship. Not fearful reverence. But love.

Laughter echoed across the garden and into heaven. The fellowship was sweet. Creator smiled as Created named each animal, exulting in every one. Together they explored the secrets of Eden and the wonder of this new friendship. But as the days passed, a growing conviction gripped the heart of Creator. A bittersweet realization that there was still more to give.

Each creature had a mate. Another of its kind. But the man was alone.

"It is not good for man to be alone. I will make a helpmate." And in that moment love was born. Not in the creation of the woman, but in the Creator's willingness to share the man. In the Creator's willingness to give.

For God so loved...he gave. Though it meant sacrificing the single-minded devotion of the man, God gave. Though it meant sharing the communion meant only for him, God gave. Though it meant the willful disobedience of man and woman would someday cost Creator the life of his dear Son, God gave.

We, too, must give if we endeavor to love. Love holds no room for selfishness. It is only in laying down our life that we find it. It is only in losing that we win.

We can learn a lot from the day Love was born.

LOVE COMES QUIETLY.
FINALLY, DROPS
ABOUT ME, ON ME,
IN THE OLD WAYS.

WHAT DID I KNOW
THINKING MYSELF
ABLE TO GO
ALONE ALL THE WAY.

Robert Creeley

And thereto I pledge my faith.

WHATEVER
YOUR LIPS UTTER
YOU MUST BE
SURE TO DO,
BECAUSE YOU
MADE YOUR
VOW FREELY TO
THE LORD YOUR
GOD WITH
YOUR OWN
MOUTH.

DEUTERONOMY 23:23

Stirring the oatmeal is a humble act....

It represents a willingness... to find meaning in simple unromantic tasks:

earning a living, living within a budget, putting out the garbage.

ROBERT A. JOHNSON

You can never be happily married to one another

until you get a divorce from yourself.

Successful marriage demands a certain death to self.

JERRY MCCANT

To repress a harsh answer, to confess a fault, and to stop

(right or wrong) in the midst of self-defense in gentle submission,

sometimes requires a struggle like life and death. But these three efforts

are the golden threads with which domestic happiness is woven.

CAROLINE GILMAN

The Tokens

IN AN ANCIENT CHURCH RITUAL,

THE RING WAS PLACED FIRST ON THE THUMB,
"IN THE NAME OF THE FATHER"; NEXT ON THE
FOREFINGER, "IN THE NAME OF THE SON"; THEN ON
THE MIDDLE FINGER, "AND OF THE HOLY SPIRIT."
IT WAS PLACED LAST ON THE THIRD FINGER, "AMEN,"
AND LEFT THERE AS A SEAL OF THE MARRIAGE BOND.

With this ring… From the earliest days, a ring has been used to seal important or sacred agreements. The unending circle symbolizes the unending love we bring to marriage.

The first known use of a finger ring in a marriage ceremony was in the Third Dynasty of the Old Kingdom of Egypt around 2800 B.C. The Egyptians believed that the circle, having no end nor beginning, symbolized eternity—which signified how long the marriage was binding.

The ring, or the "joining of hands" in some form, appears in nearly all cultures and all ages as a symbol of covenant. Hindu priests bind the bride's and groom's hands with grass. In ancient Ireland a man gave the girl he wanted to marry a bracelet woven of human hair. Before the advent of rings in Jewish marriages, a coin was broken in two and one-half given to the bride and the other to the groom as a symbol of the husband's ability to care for his wife financially. The Romans often gave their brides a heavy iron ring with the keys to their house strung upon it—"with all my worldly goods I thee endow."

As time went by, rings were made of many different materials. Peasants often wove wedding bands from hemp while other cultures formed rings from leather, carved stone, and crude metals. Gold was a favorite choice of the more affluent because of its beauty and durability.

The first known use of a Christian pledge-ring was in A.D. 860. Usually gold and without decoration, it was often engraved with the bride's and groom's names, a tradition that still continues today. Abraham Lincoln had Mary Todd's wedding ring engraved with "Love is Eternal." Another romantic husband engraved in his beloved's ring "Each for the other, both for God MWG to MEH October 21, 1890."

The wedding ring is worn on the left hand, a tradition begun by the Greeks. They believed a major artery ran from the left fourth finger straight to the heart. While that idea has been disproved, it is a lovely reminder of the commitment we make to love. An outward manifestation of an inward choice, the ring circles not only our finger, but also our heart.

And as this round
As nowhere found
To flaw, or else to sever,
So let our love
As endless prove,
And pure as gold forever.

ROBERT HERRICK
"TO JULIA"

With this ring

THIS *Ring* IS ROUND AND HATH NO END,
SO IS MY *Love* UNTO MY FRIEND.

SIXTEENTH-CENTURY VERSE

I thee wed...

I GOT A THICK *letter* FROM RUTH POSTMARKED JULY 6, 1941—

"I'll marry you," she wrote.... That night I got up to the pulpit and preached.

When I finished and sat down, the pastor turned to me.

"Do you know what you just said?" he asked.

"No," I confessed.

"I'm not sure the people did either."

...I raced right out and spent almost all of [the $165 offering] on an engagement ring with a diamond so big you could almost see it with a magnifying glass!

..."I can't wear the ring until I get permission from my parents," she said apologetically. They were away, so she sent them a telegram:

"Bill has offered me a ring. May I wear it?"

"Yes," they wired back, "if it fits."

—BILLY GRAHAM
JUST AS I AM

IT WAS SO VERY
GOOD OF GOD
TO LET MY
DREAMS COME
TRUE, TO NOTE
A YOUNG GIRL'S
CHERISHED HOPES
THEN LEAD HER
RIGHT TO YOU.

RUTH BELL GRAHAM
RUTH: A PORTRAIT

So do not worry, saying, "What shall we eat?" or "What shall we drink?" or "What shall we wear?" For the pagans run after all these things, and your heavenly Father knows that you need them. But seek first his kingdom and his righteousness, and all these things will be given to you as well. MATTHEW 6:31-33

One by one they opened the cards, carefully reading the sentiments before examining the contents. A ten-dollar bill dropped out of the first one and into Debbie's lap. "That'll get us to Saginaw!" A check here and a five there—like manna from heaven, the money drifted down, covering Debbie's lap and sliding onto the LeSabre's tan vinyl seats.

The honeymoon was everything they dreamed of and more.

When they returned to Athens to set up housekeeping, neither John nor Debbie had anything to fill the parsonage. Their possessions were few: some suitcases of clothing, a box of books from college, and assorted wedding gifts. But they were home. They nestled in with a borrowed table and two chairs and a mattress for the bedroom floor. The Lord had provided once. He would provide again.

Several weeks later John's parents called to say they were going on the road. They didn't want to put their furniture in storage. Would John and Debbie mind keeping everything at their house?

Debbie motioned for John to come to the phone. Ear to ear they listened to the proposal, grinning and nodding at each other.

"Not at all, Mom," John said generously. "Not at all."

I would rather have a crust and a tent
with you than be queen of all the world.

Isabel Burton to her husband, Sir Richard Burton

The Declaration

SO WE GREW
TOGETHER,

LIKE TO A DOUBLE CHERRY, SEEMING PARTED,

BUT YET AN UNION IN PARTITION;

TWO LOVELY BERRIES MOLDED ON ONE STEM.

WILLIAM SHAKESPEARE
A MIDSUMMER NIGHT'S DREAM

"Listen all ye that are present: Those that were distant are now brought together; those that were separated are now united."

In the Malacca Straits this is the proclamation the elder makes at the end of a marriage ceremony. Through the portal of these words a couple embarks on a great adventure, filled with romance and intrigue. The proclamation marks the end of a wedding and the beginning of a marriage.

Jesus affirmed the sanctity of marriage when he echoed God's instruction to Adam and Eve in Genesis, "For this reason a man will leave his father and mother and be united to his wife, and the two will become one flesh. So they are no longer two, but one. Therefore what God has joined together, let man not separate" (Matthew 19:5-6).

Like two children at a picnic, as newlyweds we are signed up for the three-legged race. Breathless with excitement and anticipation, we take our place at the starting line. "On your mark. Get set. Go!"

With the proclamation, we leave the altar, arm in arm. Together we begin to run, holding tightly to each other, lurching, laughing, lunging, and sometimes falling. But eventually we find the rhythm of being one, the smooth cadence of being husband and wife. And on we go, our eyes held fast to the goal, our hearts determined to reach the finish line one step at a time.

> FLESH OF
> MY FLESH,
> BONE OF MY
> BONE, I HERE,
> THOUGH THERE,
> YET BOTH
> BUT ONE.
>
> ANNE BRADSTREET

Those whom God
hath joined together,
let no man put asunder.

TWO BECOME *One.* They sat side by side in the dark, holding hands. My husband, John, didn't see them until he flipped on the switch, filling the prayer room with light.

"I'm sorry," John said. "I didn't think anyone was in here."

"Not a problem," the old gentleman said with a wink. The two sat close at one end of a pew that stretched along the far wall. He gathered his tiny, gray-haired wife a bit closer, and she smiled shyly, looking at her husband and then at the embarrassed youth pastor. John stood there for a moment, uncertain.

He'd heard about the old man, how he had once been a strapping young farmer, tilling the fields of eastern Montana from dawn till dusk. But now his body was bent and grizzled, the large ranch abandoned years ago for a small house in town. His wife fit neatly beneath his arm as each Sunday they shook John's hand after morning service. Her eyes still sparkled; her hair glowed like a white halo around her wrinkled but pretty face.

Like two puzzle pieces they fit. Like two shadows melded into a single silhouette. Differences had long ago been blended by compromise, their original diversity somehow faded into the sweet unity of many loving years. They even looked alike, their features softened by age to a near siblinglike sameness.

He poured so gently and naturally into my life
Like batter into a bowl of batter,
Honey into a jar of honey.
The clearest water sinking into sand.

✦ JUSTINE SYDNEY

John came home that night and shared the story. "I want a love like that," John said, his voice tender with emotion. Our lives had grown so busy we'd barely had time for each other. Together we prayed, asking God to help us build a love that years could not put asunder. Asking that he would make us truly one. Asking that when we grew old and gray, we'd not only resemble each other, but we'd still find time to hold hands in the dark.

John chuckled as he told me how the couple had exchanged pleasantries for a while, but at the first lull in the conversation, the old Scandinavian farmer released John politely, saying, "You can go now."

"Of course," John stuttered, backing out the door.

"Oh—and pastor?" the farmer said, smiling mischievously. "Don't forget to turn off the light."

TWO SOULS
WITH BUT
A SINGLE
THOUGHT,
TWO HEARTS
THAT BEAT
AS ONE.

ÉLIGIUS VON MÜNCH–
BELLINGHAUSEN

MY WIFE

Trusty, dusky, vivid, true,
With eyes of gold and bramble-dew,
Steel-true and blade-straight
The great artificer
Made my mate.

Honor, anger, valor, fire;
A love that life could never tire,
Death quench or evil stir,
The mighty master
Gave to her.

Teacher, tender, comrade, wife,
A fellow-farer true through life,
Heart-whole and soul-free
The august father
Gave to me.

ROBERT LOUIS STEVENSON

MY HUSBAND

If ever two were one, then surely we.
If ever man were loved by wife, then thee;

If ever wife was happy in a man,
Compare with me ye women if you can—

I prize thy love more than whole mines of gold,
Or all the riches that the East doth hold.

My love is such that rivers cannot quench,
Nor ought but love from thee, give recompence.

Thy love is such that I can no way repay,
The heavens reward thee manifold I pray.

The while we live, in love let us so persevere,
That when we live no more, we may live ever.

ANNE BRADSTREET
"TO MY DEAR AND LOVING HUSBAND"

I pronounce that they are husband and wife. . . .

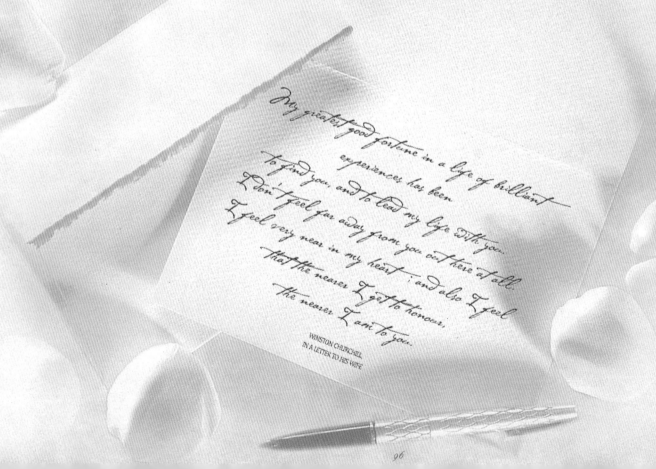

My greatest good fortune in a life of brilliant experiences has been to find you, and to lead my life with you. I don't feel far away from you out there at all. I feel very near in my heart; and also I feel that the nearer I get to honour, the nearer I am to you.

WINSTON CHURCHILL,
IN A LETTER TO HIS WIFE

Amen.

Here all seeking is over,

the lost has been found,

a mate has been found

to share the chills of winter—

now Love asks

that you be united.

Here is a place to rest,

a place to sleep,

a place in heaven.

Now two are becoming one,

the black night is scattered,

the eastern sky grows bright.

At last the great day has come!

HAWAIIAN SONG

I BLESS YOU. I KISS AND CARESS EVERY TENDERLY BELOVED PLACE AND GAZE INTO YOUR DEEP,
SWEET EYES WHICH LONG AGO CONQUERED ME COMPLETELY. LOVE EVER GROWS.

ALEXANDRA TO CZAR NICHOLAS II OF RUSSIA

Sealing the Agreement

FOUR
SWEET LIPS,
TWO PURE SOULS, AND ONE
UNDYING AFFECTION—
THESE ARE LOVE'S PRETTY
INGREDIENTS FOR A KISS.

CHRISTIAN N. BOVEE

NEVER, NEVER, *never* NEVER GIVE UP.

WINSTON CHURCHILL

PERSONAL WEDDING PHOTO SPACE

Bride's Personal Vows

RECORD THE VOWS YOU MADE AT YOUR OWN WEDDING

. . . .
. . . .
. . . .
. . . .
. . . .
. . . .
. . . .
. . . .
. . . .
. . . .

My fellow, my companion, held most dear,
My soul, my other self, my inward friend.

MARY SIDNEY HERBERT

Groom's Personal Vows

RECORD THE VOWS YOU MADE AT YOUR OWN WEDDING

....
....
....
....
....
....
....
....
....
....

I do love you...as the dew loves the flowers; as the birds love the sunshine;
as the wavelets love the breeze; as mothers love their firstborn;
as memory loves old faces; as the yearning tide loves the moon;
as angels love the pure in heart.

MARK TWAIN

SOURCES

p. 15-16   "A Dream Come True" told with the permission of Jim and Patty Porter.

p. 24   "My Life Has Been...," Paul Valéry, *The Collected Works in English*, Bollingen Series XLV, vol. 2: *Poems in the Rough*, translated by Hilary Corke (Princeton, N.J.: Princeton University Press, 1969). Copyright © 1969 by Princeton University Press, copyright renewed 1997 by Princeton University Press. Used by permission.

p. 31   "A Marriage," Michael C. Blumenthal, *Against Romance* (N.Y.: Viking-Penguin, 1987), 16. Used by permission of the author.

p. 32-34   "Come What May" told with the permission of Kim and Krickitt Carpenter, whose book, *The Vow: The Story of Kim and Krickitt Carpenter*, will be released by Broadman & Holman in 2000.

p. 56-58   "Let Me Be Your Mirror" adapted from Bill and Pam Farrel, *Love to Love You!* (Eugene, Ore.: Harvest House, 1997), 12.

p. 69   "Love Comes Quietly," Robert Creeley, *Collected Poems of Robert Creeley, 1945-1975*, (Berkeley: University of California Press, 1983), 249. Copyright © 1983 by the Regents of the University of California. Used by permission.

p. 79   "It was so very good...," Ruth Graham, *Ruth: A Portrait* (New York: Doubleday, 1997), 87. Used by permission.

p. 79   "I got a thick letter...," Billy Graham, *Just As I Am* (New York: HarperCollins, 1997), 75-76.

p. 81-82   "Sharing the Wealth" told with the permission of John and Debbie Palmer.

p. 103-105   "First Kiss" told with the permission of Stone and Gwendylann Faulkenberry.

ABOUT THE AUTHOR

JOANNA WEAVER IS A PASTOR'S WIFE, MARRIED FOR MORE THAN SEVENTEEN YEARS. SHE AND HER HUSBAND, JOHN, LIVE IN MONTANA, WHERE THEY OFTEN COUNSEL MARRIED AND ENGAGED COUPLES. THEY ARE THE PARENTS OF TWO CHILDREN, JOHN MICHAEL AND JESSICA.